Wet Specimen

Sundress Publications • Knoxville, TN

Book Editor: Erin Elizabeth Smith
Managing Editor: Krista Cox
Editorial Assistant: Kanika Lawton
Editorial Interns: Elizabeth DiGrande, Emma Goss

Colophon: This book is set in Goudy Old Style.

Cover Image: "Wet Specimen" by Rebecca Hawkes

Cover Design: Kristen Ton

Book Design: Erin Elizabeth Smith

Wet Specimen
Abigail Raley

Acknowledgements

Grateful acknowledgment is made to the editors of the following journals and magazines in which these poems, some in different versions, first appeared:

Bullshit Lit: "Poem Without You"

HAD: "DO NOT FEED THE ANIMALS" and "Ode to the Woman Who Had a 'Loud Full Body Orgasm' While the L.A. Philharmonic Played Tchaikovsky's Fifth"

Hanging Loose Magazine: "Differences from Yesterday," "The Snail," and "When Born, There Were Blue Jays"

HORNS: "Flying Fox"

Identity Theory: "M.A.S.H"

Maudlin House: "Sorry, but the T. Rex Doesn't Look Anything Like What You Think It Does"

The Offing: "Study for a Portrait"

Rejection Letters: "Sickness Swallowed Down Like Late June"

The Stone Circle Review: "Crows"

V.I.B.E. Magazine: "Lot's Wife," "Meconium Ileus," and "Ode to Fetal Deer"

Table of Contents

for Reeta

M.A.S.H.

Mansion. Apartment. Shack. House.

Logan and I have two
thousand kids. It's great. Sex isn't real.
It never was. Storks bring babies. My stork's
name is Dobi, and he's been making ten trips
a day for quite a while now. We tip him
in fish. I never turn thirteen.
I spend all my time on a project to negotiate
my way out of eating broccoli, and no one
makes me eat it. We play a game, and
no one makes fun of me when I carry
the basketball. I carry the basketball
all day long. I weave it daisy chains
and watch the hummingbirds play
tennis. I never turn fourteen.
I never bleed. Dobi brings us bruises,
but they're grapes and we eat them,
and they pop and, somewhere, the Cupid
Shuffle plays and we dance, and I always
go the right way. I'm smart like that.
I have the whole package. I'm pretty
in the way that is without lust. I wear
my church shoes and my socks
with the frills at the cuff, and I only take them off
myself. No one ever touches me. I never
turn fifteen. Men's fingers are just fingers,
not bullets, but, still, Logan holds my hand
in the park, at the train station, in the grocery.
I never turn sixteen. My heart doesn't migrate
to my throat. It all stays where it's supposed
to be inside of me. We sit in my sunset
spot at the end of the drive, and we watch

the dusk lurk and eat pepperoni, and Logan
says he loves me, and I say I love him too,
and he says that everything is magnificent
that way. I never turn seventeen. There is
no man in the alley, no man in the car,
and so, we sit all night, and Dobi comes,
and he sits beside us, and I kiss the top
of his head, and he smells like oak and trout.
We run inside because it starts to rain
human hands, heavy, down on
top of us, and not a one ever hits me. I have
a cup of cocoa. Logan puts a log on the fire,
and I admire his lack of vertigo, appreciate
his steadiness, his innocent neck, and I
never turn eighteen, and I never turn twenty,
and nothing keeps on happening, nothing
after blissful nothing, and I never go
to the room, and the dark is never so black.
I say to Logan, *I think something bad
is about to happen,* and he says *Stop
being so silly,* and I do, and the hands
come down all around us. They pound
on the roof, and I hold Dobi, and Logan reads
Where the Sidewalk Ends, and the sidewalk ends,
and the hands keep falling, and I stop being so silly.
I really do.

I.

Crow

All you need to know is that there
are birds, somewhere, birds on the line
dividing the sky in two, their talons
clutching their suspension, their highwire
kissing the moon's lap, and at the top
of the utility pole holding them taut,
keeping aloft their still bodies, there is
a nest, a nest made of my hair,
stems from my favorite rose bush,
slivers of tinsel I ripped from my cat's
jaws, just in the moment she could've
swallowed them whole, fronds
of milkweed, dried blades of grass I picked
from the lawn and discarded when, putting
them between my wet lips, they refused
to sing, but what's most important—
and this is my favorite part—
is that, at the nest's center,
there are eggs, blue as a spot
of turquoise dropped into
the river, and in them, finally,
there is the inside, the inside
I would candle with the butane lighter
I took from your coffee table
that first bright morning I woke next to your
small body, wrapped around me
like a quilt, your deep breath
hot on the fur of my lobe,
my flesh naked and without envy,
your fingers heavy and steady
and long on their course to my center,
and when you trapped yourself

inside the husk of me,
I felt hot and sweet, as simple
as nectar, as quiet as a chick
in its shell, and as you dressed
and made yourself again a person
of the world, I felt my own creature
deep and hard and new, so when
I pulled you into me and kissed
into your abyss, you cupped
the yolk of my throat in your hand
and squeezed it gently
and never let it break.

Rewilding

Once, too, my cat was feral. The raw cost:
her kittens, dead as the rotten wood I scrubbed
from the walls of the mobile home. Summer

like sewage. Kittens dead, infested. Maggots
bleeding every orifice: what it takes
to be an animal, soft in the wild.

Of course, when asked for my body
I gave. I extracted my hope in attempt
to make my skin a boundary again. I gerrymandered

me into doggy, missionary, reverse cowgirl,
was parceled into counties and jurisdictions,
named *you* and cooed into

submission. When touched, I fell
quiet, a mother curled around her
sharp, foundering obsessions.

I Give a Blowjob in the Parking Lot
of the Eggs 'N' Bacon to a Man I Knew
Briefly in My Childhood

First, there was a home, a garden, a heart-
shaped koi pond. Then, fruition, breasts,

plasma and pubis, but now pavement,
which buckles, vaporous in the humidity.
When you called, I was taken with your

proposition for *car sex*, not for the eloquence
of the message, but rather, in the hope
I could unpucker myself to intimacy.

I didn't think you meant blowjob, which here
means work. I wish I could be little again
reading in my mother's lap,

watching the koi make their circuitous routes,
pumping the heart of the pond as if
stuffed and hot with blood.

Bath

The sparsely furred round of my areola
bobs the water's murky surface. I am
melting into puddles of milk and cheese,
scraping off my heels, curds drifting in
my reflection. I am so absorbed, I hardly realize
your body over mine. Its spongy size, your
apparatus of knees, coagulated into orgasm,
toes clustered around my ears, nails in my
periphery. Honey, let me clip them. I'll show you
one gentle kindness after the next.

Aberdeen

The cows eat the grass
so the snakes don't come, but
they come. I touch your beard
in the warm summer morning,
a snake in the grass.

I touch the window
sill, I touch the light,
I touch the prospect

of five thousand pies,
a squirrel's dried hide.

You pray and say
mercy before you put
the vixen down.

You put my body down and wander
into the middle of the land.
I twist

the stem off the peach.
I say every letter
of the alphabet till it breaks.

It breaks.

Every day, Lord,

every day is the deep
of death's heavy lake.

Nadir

I'm almost ready, so wet for you, so horny,
but first the birds need hunting.
I need to watch their delicate bodies
drop out of the dawn.

I promise to do dirty things,
to bring you chickens
with their little wrung necks
lolling. Baby, I'm making

biscuits. I'm wondering about love
and all its pieces. I'm on all fours
mushing clay and moss into
my skin, playing with myself.

I'm eating mushrooms, so, maybe,
one will kill me and you will come
into the woods to find me because
once, here, you saw me befriend

a box turtle. Maybe I came looking
for him. After all, I've been gone
for so many days. So long
you've begun to imagine

fingering my briny folds.
So long that when you find me,
my face is blue and diffuse.
Sweet as a puff of fresh

tobacco on a teacake tongue.
Imagine it. Baby, imagine

the two of us, you and I,
soft and lost and filthy.

Flying Fox

It's Bat Coachella, and the nectar is fucking us up.
I give bat oral behind the bleachers of a eucalyptus
tree, crash into a newlywed couple's rich veranda, scream
up at the sea of freshly-alive stars *GIVE ME A LOVE
YOU INCIDENTAL APPARATUS OF LIGHT GIVE
ME MY LOVE*, and the soft, young couple emerges,
with their heavy boots and their rough brooms shooing,
the missus a ripe jewelweed waiting to be fingered shut.
I rocket up; I back to the mating ground, past the replete verdant
pastures, my destination predicated only on my instinct
to the shore's endless magnetism. I bust my way back
into the vortex of my brethren, and, all at once, we're
moshing. We're shitting on so many roofs, triumphant.
I am single and wet and full of cicadas, and the best night
of my life is upon me. On the way to the bat porta potty,
someone is kissing me and it doesn't matter who. I am
voracious. I want a bat to wrap around the fruit
of my love. I am culling my incessant lust, shooting
down its moonlit wings and watching it plummet,
drunk, into sleep. I whisper, *Hey, I think you're really
foxy*, and I don't mean *pest*, but, rather, that I want
the body in all its wretched animality, that I am lulled
by my mouth's wicked migration downward, that my
amygdala is plump and dewy and cruel. *Make my
mouth the warehouse for your cherub's thunder*,
I think, and semen trickles down my thin, red jowl.

Deliverance

If you saw a cannibal in the woods
        did you see me? Did you see

cherry jello viscera dribble down my chin?
        If I am blue, am I inbred

or dead in the river?
        A joke or a cry over the mountaintop?

A woman or a shriek broken clear
        into the night?

If I touch my shins with my toes,
        was it magic or disease?

If I loved the man who killed me,
        am I a devil or

only dead in the water, floating in the light
        of our singular moon?

Bottom of the River

I would abandon myself in the middle of the river
if the river was you. I would eat myself alive
if you told me to, if you didn't say my name again,
if you didn't step into the middle of the floor
and say, *Dance with me.* I would eat myself.
I would, alive, chew my fingers to nubs
because they touched your skin. I would
hook through the meat of my back and
dangle over the highest bridge, swell
like an abscess, blood shirking off
my shoulders, a new creature, lewd
with agony, crashing long into the rock
and tide, the air and the mountains
all around me, you. I would never be alone.

The Wound

Factory, smog, honeysuckle in the dew, crisp
before the working interrupt this time of rest.

Your amber ornate, mellow as cantaloupe,
toothpaste twitching on your morning tongue.

You, there, in the cut lawn, fog clung around
your ankles. These cricket homes through

which you intrude, the dawning day a silence
removed. I can still see you there in your young

shape ready to taste me as a dog
does a throbbing wound, finding

for the first time that absolutely
everything is love.

Beast

I play the game with my finger
prints singed off. I touched the hot
pan on purpose.

And why shouldn't I? Eat, I mean. Why
shouldn't I put your penny on my tongue
and shuck out all its copper juices?

Why shouldn't I, with this bulb
of acid in my spasming throat,
for the first time, crunch my tongue

between my teeth? I am standing
on the razor shore of an ocean. Maybe
it is a lake. Maybe it is the edge

of your esophagus. In every iteration
I am touching your soft inside.
There is blood in my mouth.

Skin on my teeth. Your skin
on my teeth. Your lips beneath
my lips. Your eyes under my eyes.

Tomorrow Night Jupiter Will Be Closer
to the Earth Than It Ever Has Been
or Ever Will Be for 500 Years

and the lambs will gather at the edge
of the field to look out on the dogs
with their teeth, hot mouths tilted
into the damp air, the night
with its moon and its road
made of hills, where the fox
creeps into town, leaves her musk
for me at the foot of the door.
The sky is a hole when I smell
her, and I am lost so softly
in it as you, with Jupiter lurking
above your naked head, slip
your hand beneath my blouse
and make this hollow thing of me.

II.

Suburbia

I am a tightrope of a woman.
I stand in front of the fridge
for literal decades. I made
the living room an icebox.
I'm in the shower, and it's windy.
It's a downpour, torrential
every time I try to wash
my hair. We ought to get
that fixed. The ice in the living
room is melting into the carpet,
and it's about time you and I
had a serious conversation.
I can't keep kissing and kissing
you. I don't want your tongue
or the crust that fondles it. The tooth
and then the other and the overwhelming
other again and again, their proliferation
and their smack. The pasta and the shrimp
untucking from its space as it does, too,
in the trash can in the garage. I hate it here.
I know it's my fault that the mold made
her living in our home. I know I asked
her in and sat her down and said *I love
you baby please come back to me*. It's
just not enough, waiting for someone
to feed me. It's not enough waiting
for the tundra to thaw, for the weather
to change, for you, one day, to decide
that you love me, that you could take
my body's dead bird and hold it
to your chest, lifting only the lids
of our trash can to say *I will never*

see this place again, only spitting
down to the hot pavement to cool
a place for my lithe wings, never
putting me down into that great beast.
Instead, the sun.

The Abortion

after Anne Sexton

A DVD of the first *Hangover* movie.
A half-eaten piece of blueberry pie.
Chips, Gatorade, Tylenol, a bass
guitar. One, and only one, painting.
The walls, ceiling tile, water stains,
the drain, the drain dripping.
Drain drop? At any rate, tap water.
Toilet. Two neighbors, fighting
over a TV, and, outside, a TV
in the trash. The trash, for that matter,
the crows, or were they blackbirds,
gathering leftover fries from leftover
bags from:
Rally's, McDonald's, Denny's
Wendy's, Cane's and one cat,
watching them, by the only
window, nearest the only painting.
That window, shaking at the sound.
The sound. My voice.
My voice.

Aubade with Cystic Fibrosis

there was once
a creature
that emerged
from my coffin
of a throat
and said
feed me
but i
unable to discern
her meaning
instead spat blood
down my front
and coughed
and coughed
until out flew
a thousand
lunar moths
that spun a cocoon
around my weeping
briny body
and unplugged the drip
of fluid to my heart
transforming me
into a toady obelisk
a seizing thrumming
buzz ejecting pus
in glossy globs in
misty green orbs
the dewdrops
that clung
to my ankles
stunning mornings

that didn't shake
me down
bright air
that didn't consist
of my body
just waking up

Creature from the Black Lagoon

Then, in the darkness that divides the cumbersome
morning from the sunlight's darling buzz,
in the interim, I slept at the bottom of a large,
black lake. I slept until my boundaries dissolved
and I became, at once, a series of sensation, stimuli
exploding, fissure after ruthless fissure evaporated
from my non-body, my endless entity-less, synapse,
mucking down around the bottom of the lagoon.
I was eely, sliding in and out. I opened and closed
the door that burbled at the pond's scummy end.
I pulled my not-hand up around the handle and saw
some mix between tentacle and bone, exposed.
I wanted more water in. When I opened the door,
I noticed myself azure in the morning light. I thought
on my life, then. How, soon, I would arrive to work
and sell stacks of contracts to the republic. *Poor
thing,* I thought, *with your fixed body and your
pain.* I imagined I was a school of fish, divided
and swam away.

Ripe

A man I loved
once said, in between his
tenderness, from out of
his teeth, *you have nothing*
                        to live for.

A man I loved once said
I am only waiting
        for you to die,

and when he put his hands around my
throat, it was because he wanted
my body, and if he said he loved me, it was
because he wanted to put his hands
around my throat, and when he did,
the worst part was, I crawled upon
the shoal of my happiness
and stroked its wet sands.

                You have a resentment
                        which has limited
                                the way that you love me.

I shoved my hands in up to the wrists.

He trophied me, said *you're so mature,*
but he was wrong. I was naive
in my assessments. In my process,
I was young, soft in my need.

By *mature,* he meant,
you are a fruit

I haven't yet bruised.

By *mature*, he meant

    Your body has so much space
                  to hold
your silence.

Ode to Fetal Deer

Your small body, culled beneath the jar's
collapsed glass womb. Your brine mine, too.

Your spots the shade of my pale skin chilly
with the round drip of saline. How you

sleep: like me, in the colliding world,
formaldehyde biome beetle-less. Beloved,

show me your stale serenity, how the light
penetrates the cutis, skinned, illuminating

its massive, incandescent vesicle. Combustible
sterility, your retained face cabineted behind

the heavy metal door. Child, tell
me more of why it reads: *DANGER!*

Meconium Ileus

meconium: Greek, meaning poppy
ileus: Greek, meaning twisted
meconium ileus: a thickening of the bowel, causing digestive issues,
most often seen in patients with cystic fibrosis

Tell me I was beautiful, that I was a poppy in the field
and the field was full of air and the air was clean and dreadful

and large. Tell me I was large. Tell me I pummeled
the ground. Tell me the ground was laced with minerals

that made me clean and new, that I was as old and warm
as the earth. Tell me I endured the plundering, that fire

sustained me, that I endured the sutures. Tell me, my love,
of my dream. Tell me the dream where my sickness is a bud

in a vast garden. Tell me I was a whole vegetable, a whole
fruit holding down the pain, keeping it my hostage.

Honest

The weight of my missing
bore down. Its thin leaves
leaves, like paper, stood.
Agency was an unwashed
dish. The velocity
of my cruelty. Its shape
flung out. I slept
and wished I'd wake
alone, but there he was
by morning, his heart
a stupid dove.

Lot's Wife

"As CF is caused by a faulty gene that controls the movement
of chloride and water into and out of cells, people with CF
often sweat more than people without the condition, and this
sweat contains high levels of chloride, which can crystalize
into salt visibly on the skin." –The Cystic Fibrosis Trust

"but his wife looked back from him, and she became a pillar
of salt" –Genesis 19

It is 1981, and love is a thing with fists. Love comes with cousins
and their knuckles, the back's sinew pounded, purple all the way
down to the ribs, newly budded breasts in their pink bikini pressed
hard into the hot pavement. The sun is as bright as it ever was, always

threatening its crest. Still, her gaunt skin pales the light. Her world
initiates its end, even through summer's gentle tide. God floats
across the heavy chalice of her throat like a high, bright balloon.
Her head, lifted, observes the pool, its chlorine blue and still

as a lake, dizzy in the heat. The fists remain. They steady,
spread their task. The sludge vomits up, thick and sentient,
a slack slug extracted from the fibroid's vast garden.
She spits, gags, musters onto the manufactured shore.

Pantoum as the Next Trans Child Killed
by Legislative Violence

"I was born at night, but not last night" –Kentucky
Representative Pamela Stevenson, responding to
Representative Jennifer Decker, in opposition of HB 470,
which makes illegal puberty blockers and hormone
replacement therapy for transgender children.

I was born at night, but
not last night. Not
under rapid gunfire, atop the shattered
glass illuminating my trapped-buggedness.

Not last night. Not
in the congressional hall, the capitol building
glass illuminating my trapped-buggedness.
Then again, maybe I *was* born

in the congressional hall, the capitol building
squashing me beneath her manicured thumb.
Then again, maybe I *was* born
into a body asphyxiating itself,

squashing me beneath her manicured thumb.
The lady, the representative, forces me
into a body asphyxiating itself,
and I am a child, but

the lady, the representative, forces me
under rapid gunfire. Atop the shattered
dignity of my flesh, the flashing of my life:
I was born at night, but

Poem Without You

Walked out today. Threw myself into the thick white of the morning. Bought fruit / tea / little bags of nuts / onions / one can of tomato sauce / cannellini beans / a bouquet of lilies. Contemplated throwing myself over my favorite bridge, how the light could catch my glinting body through the parting fog, the sun a blood diamond above the clouds. Anyway, I didn't. I went home. Saw my cat. Pet her round head. Fed her purée. At home, on the TV, they talked about Marquette, its minerals: Lake Superior agate, Jacobsville sandstone, the Black Rocks. I grabbed an apple and bit into it. I put frozen blueberries on my cracked skin. Thought to myself, *What I hate most about living is the future*, then wished I had a scab to worry. If, forever, I could wake and hear the shower running, smell an egg frying all on its own, walk down to the beach and see why the lighthouse was automated, how it is itself alone without a keeper, maybe I could understand this life a little more, maybe I could hear my loneliness. I made a cup of tea, and when it steeped, it was the color of Lake Superior agate, the hibiscus mocking Michigan's fertile, wealthy coast. I put one spoon of sugar in, a second, a third. I sipped and pictured breakfast, two cups of coffee on a diner table, a piece of pie with two forks.

The Crushing

It's enchanting, the way rain is celebrated in the West. Cold, glacial, and cicada-less, these rains are unlike thunderstorms in the South. They arrive and depart without sound.

Where did I read it? The description of the rain that called it a child
pummeling its sister.

Christina Olson wrote a poem wherein a judge asks a woman how she was abused. The speaker's explanation is *with fists*.

I wonder how the rain buffets the earth. What part of her body does she bring down?

Once, I crushed a snail beneath my heel. On the cobblestone path to our home, shells were indiscernible from the inset quarry rocks that lined the walkway.

Carmen Maria Machado drops a snail and notes its *white foam* frothing from the site of impact.

My heaves clenched down so deep I began to spit acidic spume. A thousand tiny snails inside me, crushing down and down until my esophagus is full of their bile.

Dying manifests not only horrific displays of mortality, but, too, delicate acts of love.

I have vomited handfuls of blood so black my mother recalled the lullaby
she sang to me in my childhood.

Wildfires gather us to the delicate miracle of rain.

Bob Flanagan said *my parents loved me even more when I was suffering.*

For the first time since October, I open the window. Across the brown lawn, a couple huddles under the awning. They grip each other tightly in the comforter they snatched from their bed. One files out into the rain, then the other. They kiss, and the rain, all around them, pummels the thawing skin of the earth.

I hum to myself *all the pretty little horses*, my shadow a dilating pupil.

Landscape with Magpies Nesting in the Blizzard

On my desk: a sliver of tangerine skin, ossified from its months
of being made.

There is a You with me. He, the You, says, *Do not be afraid,*

but he doesn't say that, not really. He really kisses me. We talk about turtles
right before. We talk about their scarlet ears. And then his hands on my
back.

My coat, off.

He does not say, *I received what I want from you and I am done.*

He says, *The dusk is coming, blue like a mangled appendage.*

He says, *The bubble's short infinity is reaching its opposite side.*

You see, I think I was bad in my life.

I think I did something wrong.

I said, *I love you* instead of *I have been peeled, made like a dressed hen.*

I said, *I want to wet your torso* and not *the hill is tonguing dawn's long violet
obelisk.*

I've spent my days in flagellation to parcel out my skin into sizeable amounts
of worry. But that isn't right. I'm sorry. Can I begin again?

I mean I looked out the window and saw the birds

and I only thought of being loved.

IV.

Ars Poetica with Cystic Fibrosis

I am not the speaker, reader.
This is not the story
about hope, about those
who come home, light as air.
This is about my hate.
I hate, I seethe, I lie.
I turn against my body,
lame, wet, stomach choked
with shit, thick lips
that lie about death,
that she was a woman
I kissed, in the end,
my friend that fingered
the close of my crumpled
body. Oh, she,
monument to which I prayed
and kissed and kissed,
slept next to every night,
comfortable in my fate.
I'd make you believe
I was a metaphor
for my skin's excretions.
Reader, I am not. I am ill
and heavy and burdensome.
Death is not a woman, not
a monument. Hear me.
I lied. I am finished
with the story. Go elsewhere. Hope
otherwise. This is the truth:
I am dying, and dying is
the end of the world.
I have fallen down

the dark hole and climbed
out selfishly, clawed
like a maggot when
its apple is sufficiently
raped. *You kiss
your children*, I could say.
*You tell them you love
them*, but what love?
What good?

Ode to You Who Have Washed the Good Earth Clean

You, who have shined my eyes into ornamental
spoons and, like sunlight, donned a brilliance
purifying and complete. I have been stupefied,
bludgeoned into elemental sediment: hair, dust,
blood. You who have obliterated the membrane
of my lust, who have guided me through every
alley blindly and with unsanctioned love, you,
who in your clarifying tenderness, found beauty
in the maggot, in the fox skin,
in the cigarette and the street-side vomit
and the Vape Nation you, O, you
who have stroked me in the cold wind, you
for whom my heart has sided with extravagance,
you have precipitated all, so my life around me,
like a river, rushes with the purity of you.

Intubation

Not a cloud darkened the heaven
under which he found my body's wound
and entered, a mirror that stood seamless
against the sky's complete blue and bound
my chest, pressed the pus into a warm
swarm, alive liquid neon. I was a woman
on her back, ribbing through lilac mornings,
drowned with my feet on the topsoil.
Fruitful as oil. Air compressed into
its own undone animal.

The New Sensation

I have been thieved out of my body,
elixered into an orgy of sensation. Light
and motion are all that remain. Always
the pain. Constancy. Dependable friend
of the fever. Insolence. Waste.

Lord, give me the new sensation. Renew
the rug of my tongue to its gentle familiar.
Grind my pharynx out of its serrations.
Make me a nubile cyborg, an apparatus
of stimuli. Give me shape again. I am
a blank field. Clarify my hill.

Omens

How the car rode, there, past puddles
of splashed pedestrians. How, on
that drive, the hawk snatched the bunny.
How it eyed me as I itched in my
saddle Oxfords, my dress too cool.
How I dreamt of hail and there
was hail the very next day. How I dreamt
of my mother's death and drew conclusions.
How a home becomes a place
where a woman becomes a girl. How I
missed the monumental growth into my
body, pleaded against my afflicted edges
and then dressed myself and gladly went to prom.

The Snail

My labia became a delicate lamb I cupped between
my thighs, and in my dreams, men made of me
an undisturbed wilderness. Sleep was a flight

into myself, where my insides remained pink and intact
like the earthworm before the shovel's heavy apocalypse
divvies her in half. It was the beginning of my mission

to find my girlhood, which had fallen behind the task
of pleasure, which was different from the pleasure
of my abuses, which were more like mosses

that spread across the lattice of my body,
and like me, opened, algal bruises greening my cheeks.
There was a lot of blood on me then.

And I was its witness, stripped below the waist
beneath the cloud-covered moonlight, mammary canopy
that refracted me, touched my masticated bowel.

Sickness Swallowed Down Like Late June

I'm on my back, and the rain nakeds my
already taut skin, wilts the now-hard bulbs
of my nipples, melts each goosebump bud of spring.

When I say magic, I mean
I stepped into a puddle and fell in
up to my waist before my toes kissed

the mud. When I say mercy, I mean
no snake was at that bottom. Summer
blesses me again and again, always plenty

of tomatoes. If I find a boulder, I stand on it
just to stand. I have no need to look out
at anything. It is June, and there is time.

My monstera weeps for all the rain. On dry
days, which are few and far between,
there is a moon so bright it pinks,

blushes at my pubic bone, at my elbow,
warm in its shaft, and I fly, open and
fleshy toward the lake. I ripple through

the trout. In my chest, a swarm of gnats,
orchestral, languid in the heat of my ribbing,
only now waking from their evening slumber,

collapsing and furring my nodes with their
song. The rain backs, it drools
down my heavy brow. I am not in love

with anyone.
My bones itch, searching
for their way out.

Differences from Yesterday

after Brian Blanchfield, after James Schuyler

The bright air, shirking off my shoulders, rapid through
the lilies of day. The day white and bouncy, like
detergent, scent booster, a bleachless load. How a mother

pulls in her son and presses her lips directly to his ear
and stills his writhing body in the public secrecy
of a crowded room. The spring, in short, finally making

its way all up and up to the mountaintop. The door
I hold for respectable men, my new shoes cutting
little holes in my heels. My friend who was once

only my friend, but is now someone's mother
on the phone trading the dailiness of her life for comfort,
her new voice tired and kept. *It just hurt my feelings,* she says

so softly I cannot recall her raucous attitudes, her
splendid way of waving a bottle of Jose Cuervo
righteously above her head in threat to *pull up*

*to that bitch's house and show her what the fuck
I mean.* These are the little losses of the new day.
I do not want to leave the bright aperture of this

morning. My professor's son is doing capoeira.
He is in front of me, saying he wrote a whole page
today in ten minutes flat. *Wow,* I say, *tell me more.*

Sorry, But the T. Rex Doesn't Look Anything Like What You Think It Does

She's actually skinny. She's on Ozempic, enduring
her small apocalypse: too many jokes about her tiny
arms. She's had a bad day. If you knew anything

about the T. Rex, you'd know that her favorite
band is Portishead, that she listens to Glory Box
for hours at a time. Some nights, that's all she does.

She sings until she sleeps, until there's nothing
left inside but the evaporating dark and piles
of uncooked eggs. In her nightmares, she drowns

her babies in her milk. *I just want to be a woman*
she sings, and it's not how you're envisioning.
Whatever you're imagining is wrong. There's

so much you'll never know. But that's it, isn't it?
How we come into these bodies. The day you
were born, even, a lesion. Your screaming mouth

wide as your foundering hope. You, too, a carnivorous
bird, wriggling in the bright room of your skin. Within,
the simple, stunning artifacts of your bones, untouched
through all those mountains of exquisite flesh.

Trapped in the Conga Line, I Ruminate on Intimacy

My press-on nails frame the stranger's
long, black ponytail, and, at once, I am aware of touch,
aware of how my gaze flits downs around his blades,

which shoulder, shrouded by the thick, crepe canvas
of his t-shirt. Deep beneath the crowded compression
of my fingers, his round muscles, warm and firm

as pumpkin vines, squirm in tandem, writhe so I talon on,
trip behind him, proximity distended and collapsed,
his body a hatchet slashing the air around us, his slim frame

a brood of towering doors. My hands on his body say, *Come
home*, say, *You're tense*, say, *Let me move you.*
What majesty, this conga of ours. All we've ever needed

is a reason. Give us time and its magnificent adornments.
We will, unfleetingly and without hesitation,
touch each other through the dark.

Ode to the Woman Who Had a "Loud Full Body Orgasm" as the L.A. Philharmonic Played Tchaikovsky's Fifth

I think you are much like Spring.
How, one day, the tree is budless and
then all at once, without explanation,
dancing in its pink devotion. The wet,
delicate dawn lighting its fertile
detonation. You are like the boisterous
squirrels hurling themselves
before my car's velocity, darting
to propitious lovers, violable, sticky,
ready to be shown and shown again. You,
shadow woman, hole shape, light cut
off, you and your body's vast excretion
stopped an orchestra, led it out of its
theme into your softness, your ticklish
flesh, thighs polarized by your desire.
You in your exuberant body, halting
the snow. You in all your intimate pieces
finally strung together like a blackberry
or the bear cub footing at his mother's
womb, fairy fingers hooding hooves,
my purple tips when I have been about
the field, plucking from the brush those
plump cherubs, slipping them between
my lips, open, like yours. Yes, when
I remember you and your thrumming body,
I remember the way that animals will always be.

April

There is a jar in my hand, one with a glass
sunflower blown into it on two sides, raised up
so that I run my thumb along its braille. It once
held a drooping sunflower. *I thought,* they said,
you could use this. On account of everything.
At the sunflower's center, a ring reads
across the fingertip like a nipple
at the center of its areola.
On account of everything, they said.
I tweak the break in the window's screen,
the wires dug out, I assume, by some nesting
pecking creature, plenty in the crevice
where their nest is kept, riding out the blizzards.
My cat's tail twitches. She cuts an ember eye
across at me, and I know that, over time,
the thing that burns hardens into a steady
receptacle from which you can drink
your sweet wildflower tea.

V.

Anglerfish

I buy enough for myself and the mouth,
which begins at my ribs, an onslaught
of tongue and maw, wide with desire
for my fingers, gentle, wet with salsa,

hummus, burrata, ranch. That night,
in the tub, I smear a lube of food
across my distended end. The mouth
talks, says, *Thank you* and *I love you.*

I, too, was once an animal, infested
with thirst. How my wild sense crawled,
a kudzu that grappled out of my navel,
down to where his tongue made

a perfect marble of my lust, clear concentric
circles. In certain light, his penis wilted
like a sunflower heavy with rain. I glom
on a lob of Philadelphia, chive and onion,

massage it into my skin, and deep within
swells a crest of fresh ejaculate. I gasp
for my body, its before glistening like iron
rimming the unbroken hymen of some

brilliant lake. *Is everything alright?* it asks,
and though it knows the answer, I do
the manufactured kindness. *Of course,* I say.
What would you like next?

Dream Record

The center of the dream was made of hands.
His fingers grew long and collapsed into mine
as if passing through some endless corridor.

His collar rippled beneath the weight
of his wide jaw. Fabric hung down
around his slender waist like a cat belly

slit open or a womb, but the hands moved
upward. I want to say they slithered, but
even that was wrong. He tentacled into

fibrous tendrils that fascinated
on the menagerie of flesh about me:
wrists, throat, thighs. He was a symphony

of touch, a demonstration of my desire, the wish
that I could be a hole hunger distilled into
and filled plump as a dumpling, a leaky,

erudite receptacle. I knew the myth
was all around me, and when I told him
he was only my dream, he grew angry like a man.

He rustled into singularity. Tried to pull out
my eyes or else force his slimy digits in,
the pinwheels of my cornea exposed like

rosebuds virginal with insects. It was a violence
so serene, complete, and perfect that when I woke
alone, I did not trust my isolation. I checked

the closets and the beds, as if I were a child.
How different he seemed, then, in those dark
hours, the morning an accruing contusion.

Now, I can only think of his hands.
How I would creep, like him,
on all my limbs for love.

Study for a Portrait
after Francis Bacon

The before was a great abeyance.
It had no face to cluster open,
no pomegranate clutches
of muscle to thud hard
against the hallway's serene
linoleum sea. It was a fantasy
we managed, the impossible silence
of our complete life, but after
fantasy appears the restless
digression of fact: his cheek,
peonied. The fat spume settled,
like dew, against the wall. The jelly
of his bright, violet eyes.
His body what it always was,
a simple fact of spring.

Black Bile

Do not imagine the bile as tar, but as the circumference
of an unclosing wound, that is: introitus, or *go
within*, a dispatch into the corpse's infinite dusk.
At the middle, the bile is as black as the center
of an open door. Black, not like the goat, but the tunnel
that remains when the bolt has performed its action.
Silence sucking the skin to crocuses. The gullet's
chronic laceration galloping to its glottal conclusion.
Black, not as the night that shrouds whatever lurks there,
beyond the uncurtained window, imbibing the sight
of you, in your epidermis, making love. No, the bile
inside is as black as the cornea through which the eye,
unceasing, restless in its hunger, devours the light.

The Uninhabitable

Alone, in my skin, again. Dawn's split
fragments on me. Windows burnished
with light. Everything odd
and immovable: the walls, my legs.

All I do is wonder of him, his interior,
his build. How globs of him worm out.
How his blood runs gently and then

hardens the space above his chest,
a muscle wilding so that the air itself
retracts, vibrates with him, in tandem.

Sleep is ardent in him, consumptive.
I want an inside, too, like his. An
inner field so dazzling and ruby

that my placid cheeks radiate
with life. His body, near mine,
is inhabited and dormant,
the pleasant stink of his sweat.

Squall

Every morning, the birds churn.
To me, they look a sea. I appreciate
their thin bodies the way a cat might,

challenging the weight of their bones
against mine, their density. Why choose
this place? How long ago?

Is this the only land now where,
after all these years, they can find
their love again? And where do they

put their feet, I mean, when making
children? How do they hold their
wings? I watch the flock churn

while he touches me, their nearly
colliding bodies making use of all
that space. His hand postures one thigh

open, then the other. My stomach wide
and flat as a saucer. The birds flurry,
their high backs furring the air.

High Pulp

I am chewing when I hear of the minister's death.

The only words are *road* and *fencepost.*

I touch my skin and imagine, in its place, less than air.

The orange's slivers find their unpleasant crevices and stick.

Later, in the still, warm dark, I say, *Take me,* say, *Take me on the balcony and let everyone see that you love me.*

In prayer, too, the body yields.

The jaw masticates its fragments.

In front of the open window, I drop my towel, my body clean in the light.

I want them to see us, so they know we are real.

On the balcony, the hung angel's stained glass shatters the wind.

I imagine under but can't picture what I know.

I am afraid to die alone, without you.

I sip the sludge to busy my lips from the shape of the word

impale.

The Universe Is Not Locally Real,
and the Physics Nobel Prize Winners Proved It

after Gabrielle Calvocoressi

You didn't know I saw you, but I did.
I was watching when, over the top

of the playset, a fight cracked into a murder
of crows. Mother, I saw aggression so flighty

it became a bird. I watched the gun umber
in his torso, dangle from his uvula, knock

about and drop down into his stomach.
I'm trying to tell you, he said, and I felt

the weight of his trying. I felt the whole
world waiting for him to try. A particle

behaves differently when you're watching
it. That's why the universe is no longer

real. Because sometimes
smallness strikes

the one it loves. On the other side
of the fence, the children silence their graves.

The headstones do nothing. The headstones
are an example of the predictable, are an example

of the known. So known: this death
that needs no watching. Consistent

with its lips. You didn't know it, but I heard
you whisper, *Stop stop stop.* You were

speaking, even though you didn't feel my gaze.
You'd be saying it all the same even

if I never was. Even then, here you'd be
all these years, still real.

American Pastoral

Outside, there is finally an angel. We touch
every eye. We count its teeth, tie it up, take

it in. Nothing is new in the old world,
so we get dressed. We go to the festival.

Up high, the flag buffets the long roof
of a very wide building.

Those who wish for the angel do not
see him. I throw a ping pong ball

into the goldfish bowl. Someone told
me to. I get the fish now. He will survive.

Across the street, a man has been smoking.
A cherry kisses his oxygen tank.

The white sky belches orange.
Our angel says, *Do not be afraid,*

but we don't hear him. We are far away,
touching each other in the parking lot.

Ode to Botfly

First, the fat,
    yielding to
        a thick purse
    of pearls.
        Somewhere,
an orifice,
    its suction.

Two sides
    of the same mouth

    kiss.

Do you feel it?
    This love, this
steep hill
    of skin?
A hole
    a child
        emerges from.

    One creature
becomes
        another's
    womb.

Ultrasound

The body is an unfortunate consequence
of sex. There should be a better way
to move. A way to gather, skinless as air, and
slink across supine territories verminous, virile

as a fruit bat. To be other than the creature one
has always been, all these years, soft and loose,
thick as liquid dripped onto porcelain rims, brimmed
with tears that gully, like rain, in the alleyway

above the tongue, the roof of the mouth stunned
with their heavy little feet, dense as neutron
stars. Trappings, these hands that fondle florals into
sensory equations, this tongue as thick as leather,

these eyes through which I see the duration of my life
and pity it, wrap it around me, latent as an unrung bell.

But Heaven

for Brian David

I was far from you and getting farther. The open
air around me folded. I knew the earth would never

be renewed. All was too putrid. The navel oranges,
radishes, tobacco leaves. So many dead squirrels

that summer, not smashed flat, but dumpling
round, animable, even. I wanted to lift the littered

bodies to my cheeks, to thumb their plump tummies,
but they remained. I began to speculate a blight.

I was away, and nothing could return.
No grave rose in the foreseen resurrective tides.

The fierce path home still trundled
fast past eviscerated deer. Banal decapitations,

sawed-off horns. The hill's wall
became a clavicle, bending. Bone dust odored

the road. I couldn't touch you anymore. Your thighs
went on in their intimate opacity, smoothed

by the firm cotton of your underwear. Your linen
shirts skirted your exposed heart, a parabola,

and the distant, shrouded opals of your kneecaps,
which once bent as you shucked me to my center,

92

were lost among the kissed-clean pews.
My love, let me tell you of the violet sky, the haze

which smuggled morning on its back. Let me
tell you how, in spite of all this loss around us,

I gazed. I thought of you.
I smiled.

DO NOT FEED THE ANIMALS

Lilac, the sun, eastward, blushy as the wound
that divvies my breast, organs gathered,

lush, into bushels of hydrangeas,
budded at the lungs, immature and vernal,

dewy as oysters in the half shell, eyes soupy
with cataracts, my sewn-shut mouth moonless

silent as the satellite above the A-frame
Dairy Queen where, once, you fed

a fawn vanilla soft serve from the cone. I
said for the first time, then, that I loved you

and warm air rushed around me,
your equinox unyielding and vital.

Even now, I bet some girl is working
at the window, making change, humming

as she dumpsters the trash. You touch your lips
to my breast so the blood clumps out like colostrum,

and even though we cannot hear them, I promise you
somewhere, the katydids are singing.

When Born, There Were Blue Jays

Mother, diarist, marked them.

Saw a jay today, she wrote.

Chatter in the trees.
Breath staggering the lung's canal.

God, it was beautiful and terrible,
the body making sound.

Never take you anywhere, she wrote.

The neighbor's baby had a spinal tap.

The face, when strained enough,
illuminates its halo. Dome corona.

Prickle where the pleasure was none.

An infant's skull is soft as a hernia
noosed through its pelvic lattice,
soft before the viscera is stuffed in.

Bone fingers the middle. Pleasure
where the bruise fruits, cerulean.

These orifices, finally, rendered.

They have been a comfort to me all this time
she wrote, *and they have been,*
I swear to God, a comfort.

Thank You

I'd like to thank my mentors—Brian Blanchfield, Sean Hill, and Keetje Kuipers—for their endless and unwavering support for my work. Without them, this book would not have been possible. Thank you, as well, to Gabrielle Calvocoressi, whose generative writing workshop at *The Kenyon Review* prompted the poem "When Born, There Were Blue Jays."

I'd also like to thank my dear friends whose work has inspired me and encouraged me throughout the development of this book, namely Nik Moore, Marko Capoferri, Kalani Padilla, Erin O'Regan White, Lauren Tess, and many others.

Thank you to my editor, Erin Elizabeth Smith, who has read this book through its many iterations and made it what it is today. Many thanks, as well, to Sundress Publications and my incredible team of editors and designers, whose dedicated and generous work has made the production of this book not only possible, but enjoyable. Thank you to my fabulous press mates, Dani and Kay, who have been my faithful companions on this journey.

Thank you, finally, to my family and friends. I love you all very dearly.

Notes

"M.A.S.H." refers to a paper and pencil fortune-telling game.

The concept of "Flying Foxes" is taken from Deborah Bird Rose's book *Shimmer: Flying Fox Exuberance in Worlds of Peril* , wherein Rose describes oral sex as a component of flying fox mating habits.

"Jupiter is Closer to the Earth Than It Ever Has Been or Ever Will Be for 500 Years" refers to the astronomical event in September 2022.

"Creature from the Black Lagoon" takes its title from the 1954 horror sci-fi character from the film of the same name.

The etymological roots and definitions in "Meconium Ileus" are all taken from Merriam-Webster.

The first epigraph of "Lot's Wife" is taken from The Cystic Fibrosis Trust's webpage "Sweat and Cystic Fibrosis," and the second epigraph is taken from Genesis in the Authorized King James Version of *The Bible.*

"Pantoum as the Next Trans Child Killed by Legislative Violence" takes its epigraph from a recording of Pamela Stevenson, which was recorded and transcribed in the NPR article "Bans on medical care for trans youth are moving quickly through the state legislatures."

The Christina Olson reference in "The Crushing" comes from her book *The Anxiety Workbook.*

The Carmen Maria Machado reference in "The Crushing" comes from her book *In the Dream House.*

The Bob Flanagan reference in "The Crushing" comes from his poem "Why."

"All the Pretty Little Horses," also called "Hush-a-Bye," is an American folk tune and lullaby.

"Differences from Yesterday" takes its concept and name from Brian Blanchfield's journaling practice, inspired by James Schuyler.

"Sorry, But the T. Rex Doesn't Look Anything Like What You Think It Does" takes its title from a 2023 article in *New Atlas*.

"Ode to the Woman Who Had a 'Loud Full Body Orgasm' as the L.A. Philharmonic Played Tchaikovsky's Fifth" references the 2023 *New York Post* article "Woman has a 'loud and full body orgasm' during LA Philharmonic concert."

"Study for a Portrait" is an ekphrastic poem that references the painting series "Study for a Portrait" by Francis Bacon.

"The Universe is Not Locally Real, and the Physics Nobel Prize Winners Proved It" takes its title from a 2022 article in *Scientific American*.

About the Author

Abigail Raley is a poet from Bowling Green, Kentucky. Her work has appeared in *The Offing, HAD, Hanging Loose Magazine, Stone Circle Review, Identity Theory*, and elsewhere. She holds an MFA from the University of Montana and is a PhD candidate at Case Western Reserve University.

Other Sundress Poetry Titles

Hound Triptych
Dani Janae
$17.95

Unrivered
Donna Vorreyer
$17.95

Pork Fluff
Tiffany Hsieh
$17.95

The Parachutist
Jose Hernandez Diaz
$16.00

Burns
SG Huerta
$17.95

Death Fluorescence
Julia Bouwsma
$20.95

Still My Father's Son
Nora Hikari
$17.95

Florence
Bess Cooley
$16.00

DANGEROUS BODIES/ANGER ODES
stevie redwood
$16.00

Spoke the Dark Matter
Michelle Whittaker
$16.00

Good Son
Kyle Liang
$16.00

Slaughterhouse for Old Wives Tales
Hannah V Warren
$16.00

Back to Alabama
Valerie A. Smith
$16.00

Grief Slut
Evelyn Berry
$16.00

Nocturne in Joy
Tatiana Johnson-Boria
$16.00